Making + MATH + Work

When Does a Line Become a Shape?

BY JOY VISTO

CREATIVE EDUCATION
CREATIVE PAPERBACKS

Published by Creative Education and Creative Paperbacks
P.O. Box 227, Mankato, Minnesota 56002
Creative Education and Creative Paperbacks
are imprints of The Creative Company
www.thecreativecompany.us

Design and production by Liddy Walseth
Art direction by Rita Marshall
Printed in the United States of America

Photographs by Corbis (Corbis, Emely), Dreamstime (Rangizzz), Getty Images (Andy Crawford), iStockphoto (Aleksangel, Bonerok, bpalmer, Petr Malyshev, onurdongel, OSTILL, Nathan Smith, tovovan, ZU_09), Shutterstock (Amero, Alexander Bark, blinkblink, indigolotos, LittleMiss, Gines Valera Marin, Arkady Mazor, tuchkay)
Vector illustrations by Donny Gettinger

Library of Congress Cataloging-in-Publication Data
Visto, Joy.
When does a line become a shape? / Joy Visto.
p. cm. – (Making math work)
Includes bibliographical references and index.
Summary: A helpful guide for understanding the mathematical concepts and real-world applications of geometry, including classroom tips, common terms such as segments, and exercises to encourage hands-on practice.
ISBN 978-1-60818-574-0 (hardcover)
ISBN 978-1-62832-175-3 (pbk)
1. Geometry—Juvenile literature. I. Title.

QA445.5.V57 2015
516—dc23 2014034727

CCSS: RI.5.1, 2, 3, 8; RI.6.1, 2, 3, 4, 5, 6, 7; RST.6-8.3, 4, 6, 7

First Edition HC 9 8 7 6 5 4 3 2 1
First Edition PBK 9 8 7 6 5 4 3 2 1

№ 4

When you think about mathematics, you probably think about a class at school where you do **calculations** and answer word problems. But have you ever thought about math being all around you? It's in every shape and pattern you see. It's in every song you hear. It's in every game you play and any puzzle you solve! The first mathematicians realized this, and they looked for ways to prove it—to show how order and reason could explain much about life as they knew it. Sometimes this was easy to do. But other times, people just didn't get it. Even some of the most intelligent people in history have struggled with math: Albert Einstein once wrote to a child, "Do not worry about your difficulties in Mathematics. I can assure you mine are still greater."

So how can you use whatever you know about math in everyday life? When you ***classify*** the insects that you see on the playground, *measure* the length between two cities on a map, or *circle* a question you don't understand on your homework, you are using math! In such cases, you are using a type of math known as geometry. This is one of the oldest branches of mathematics, and it is concerned with the shapes all around you. *When does* geometry become evident in your life?

EUCLID'S BUILDING BLOCKS

GEOMETRY IS THE MATHEMATICS OF MEASURING THE EARTH. More than 2,000 years ago, the ancient Greeks looked at the shapes in the world around them and wanted to systematically capture what they saw. One of the first mathematicians to do this in a formal way was Euclid of Alexandria. He discussed his own ideas and those of mathematicians before him in 13 books called *Euclid's Elements*. These books formed the basis of geometry, and many of Euclid's ideas are still taught in classrooms today.

A 17TH-CENTURY PAINTING OF EUCLID EMPHASIZES HIS SCHOLARLY PURSUITS.

Euclid centered his work on five postulates, or statements that are believed to be true without requiring proof. Over the years, the truth of the fifth postulate has been questioned. However, the geometry you learn accepts the fifth postulate to be true, just as Euclid did. Euclid also had five **common notions** that he believed to be true for numbers as well as shapes. With only these 10 axioms, or basic assumptions, Euclid was able to create 465 new ideas about geometry! You still learn about Euclid's ideas today and honor

his work by calling the subject Euclidean geometry.

Euclid started his study of geometry with two basic shapes—the most basic shapes that you know—the line and the circle. According to Euclid, all other shapes can be constructed using only these two. A line is the simplest of shapes, defined as a straight path that goes on forever.

One idea that is commonly studied in geometry is how lines interact with or relate to each other. Some lines are parallel to one another, meaning they never cross each other. Where have you seen lines that look like this? How about railroad tracks? Do you know for sure they will never cross? To be certain, mathematicians can use a couple of different methods, or tests. They may test to make sure that the lines are always the same distance apart. In the United States, with the building of the Transcontinental Railroad, the government set the width of the tracks at 4 feet, 8.5 inches. Such a uniform width ensured that the tracks could never get closer together.

INTERSECTING LINES ARE FOUND EVERYWHERE, ESPECIALLY IN TRANSPORTATION MAPS.

Another method of determining parallel lines involves the use of perpendicular lines. Lines that are perpendicular intersect at 90-degree angles. Two perpendicular lines resemble a plus sign or a lowercase *t*. Where have you seen perpendicular lines? Think back to those railroad tracks from earlier. Between the two pieces of track, there are other pieces connecting them called ties. If the tie is placed between the two pieces of track so that it is perpendicular to both of them, then the tracks are parallel. And if every tie on the length of the track is perpendicular, the tracks will always be parallel.

Geometry is about so much more than lines, though! It's tough to construct shapes with just lines alone—especially if lines are supposed to go on

TWO PERPENDICULAR LINES RESEMBLE A PLUS SIGN OR A LOWERCASE *t*

forever. Consider the railroad example again. Because the tracks will come to an end at a station when there isn't any more use for them, they cannot be described as true lines. To handle such limitations and to aid in the construction of figures, Euclid used pieces of lines, such as rays and segments.

What do you think would happen if you took a scissors to a line and cut it in half? Or what if you cut a piece out of it? What new shapes would you get? Cutting a line creates an endpoint, or a point that represents a stopping place. Making one cut in an imaginary line creates one endpoint. Cutting it again to keep a line from going forever creates a second.

A ray, a part of a line that has one endpoint but goes forever in the other direction, is formed by cutting a line in half. Rays are used to form angles, which are key to making shapes. An angle is formed by two rays that share an endpoint. Angles are everywhere!

The first thing to remember is that perpendicular lines intersect at angles measuring 90 degrees. Those 90-degree angles are called right angles. When you think of a right angle, you probably think of a corner. Look at a piece of paper: each corner is a right angle. Now look at the ceiling or at a window. What do you think would happen if you were in a room where the ceiling and walls did not meet at perfect right angles? Would you want to live in that room? To show a right angle in a picture, mathematicians put a little box at the corner. This symbol tells you that your angle is exactly 90 degrees.

Carpenters work hard to make sure they create right angles. A line is always 180 degrees, and a ceiling is essentially a line. When a wall and ceiling are perpendicular, they meet at two identical right angles. Those two angles are **congruent**. If the angles were not congruent, the ceiling would tip one way or another. Do you think it would tip forward or backward?

Right angles are important to our everyday life. But so are two other types of angles. The first is an acute angle, an angle with a measure smaller than 90 degrees. The other type of angle is an obtuse angle. This angle measures greater than 90 degrees (a right angle) but less than 180 degrees (a line). Think about the letters you make while writing. Which letters have obtuse angles? Do any have more than one type of angle? Some letters, such as *c* or *o*, don't have any angles.

Angles are measured using a device called a **protractor**. To use a protractor, one side of the angle must line up with the zero line on the protractor. The intersection point of the two sides

PROTRACTORS, L-SHAPED SQUARES, AND RULERS ARE COMMON MEASURING TOOLS.

(called the vertex), always sits at the origin spot in the middle of the base. The other side of the angle points to its measure. Protractors often give two different numbers that could be possible for a measurement. It's up to you to decide which is the correct measure.

Knowing the type of angle you are looking at will help you measure it. Of the two different measurements, one is always less than 90 degrees and the other is always more than 90 degrees. Practice measuring the angles shown on the protractors below. Before you get started, see if you can identify the type of angle you have. This will help you decide which number to give as an answer.

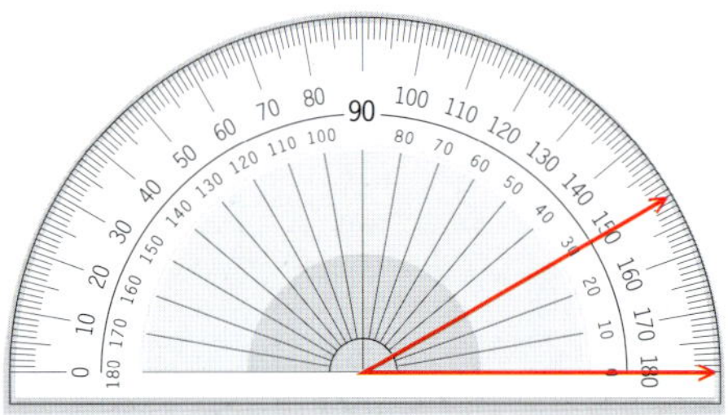

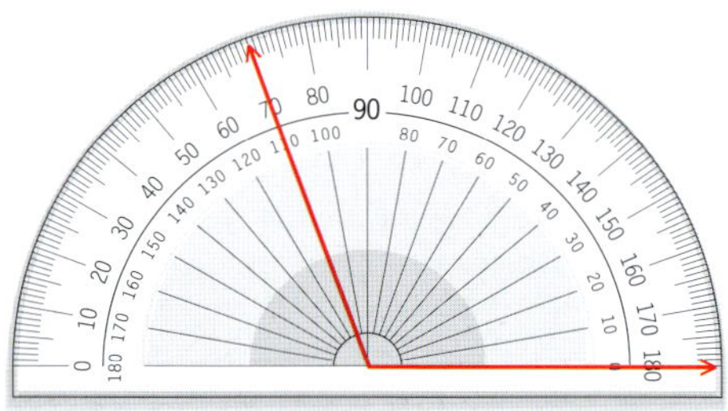

*

Angles are only part of each shape, though. Think back to the original line that was cut in half. By cutting it once, you were able to make a ray and construct angles. Cutting it again will enable you to make another of the geometry building blocks: a segment is a part of a line with two endpoints. Picture a segment as a road on a map, where the two cities connected by the road are the endpoints. Segments—unlike lines—can be measured and compared. Euclid did much of his work using segments. In fact, because the concepts of numeric values did not exist in his day, he used lengths of segments to represent any numbers.

You still use the length of segments, especially for measuring distances, but you also use segments as pictures. They serve as the sides of angles, especially in shapes. In fact, when you use these two building blocks of angles and segments, you are replicating Euclid's own methods. You, too, can measure the earth with the help of geometry. To get started, though, you will need to examine different shapes.

**Answer Key: Problem A*

FIGURE IT OUT!

Hyperbolic Geometry

Euclid's fifth postulate says that through any point not on a given line, there is only one line that is parallel to it. Another type of geometry called hyperbolic geometry argues that there are infinitely many lines that are parallel. Picture trying to do geometry on the bell of a trumpet. While Euclidean geometry may work better for you in school, a theoretical physicist will be more inclined to follow the rules of hyperbolic geometry.

THREE SIDES, THREE ANGLES

THE MOST BASIC SHAPE THAT MATHEMATICIANS CAN BUILD IS THE TRIANGLE. Triangles are **polygons** with three sides and three angles. From musical instruments to American currency, you have probably seen triangles in many objects and places.

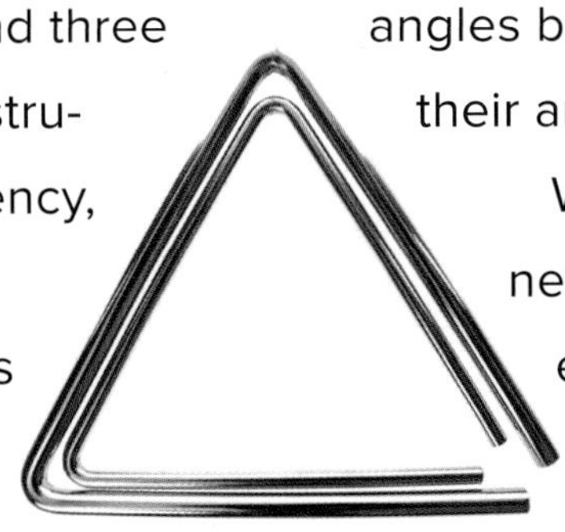

Triangles used as percussion instruments and the triangles on the back of a dollar bill are both equilateral (having three sides that are congruent) and equiangular (having three angles that are congruent). Mathematicians use words such as "equilateral" and "equiangular" to describe triangles based on their sides and their angles.

When triangles are neither equilateral nor equiangular, then you have to use different terms to describe them. Only when all three sides are congruent is a triangle equilateral. A triangle with two congruent sides is called isosceles. This classification was originally presented by

A PYRAMID'S TRIANGULAR FACES MEET AT A POINT, OR VERTEX.

Euclid. In an isosceles triangle, the two congruent sides are called legs, while the third side is the base. The final classification, scalene, describes a triangle that has no congruent sides.

The same designations for angles apply to triangles, when it comes to classifying them according to their angle measures. If a triangle has three angles that are all less than 90 degrees, then the entire triangle is acute. If one of the angles is 90 degrees, then it is a right triangle. If one of the angles is greater than 90 degrees, then you have an obtuse triangle.

All triangles can be classified using a side classification and an angle classification. In fact, certain classifications naturally fit together. For instance, any triangle that is equilateral is also equiangular. Can you describe each of the triangles below using the classifications discussed so far?

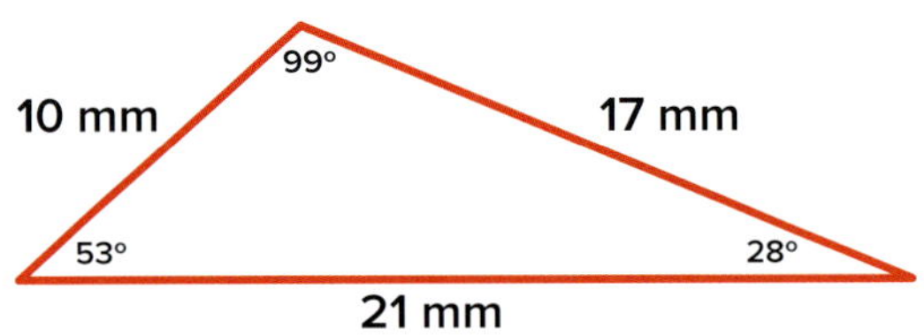

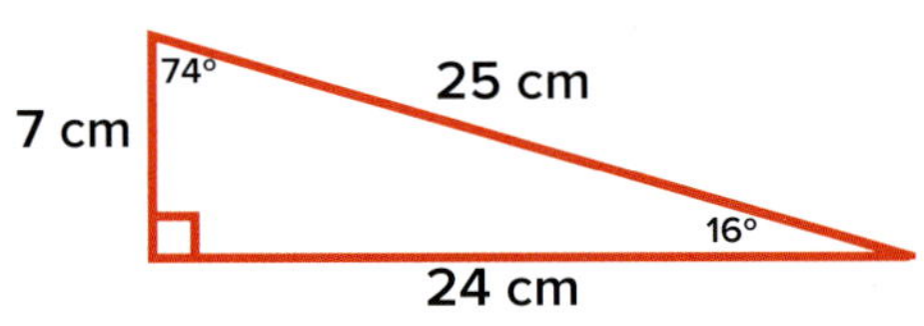

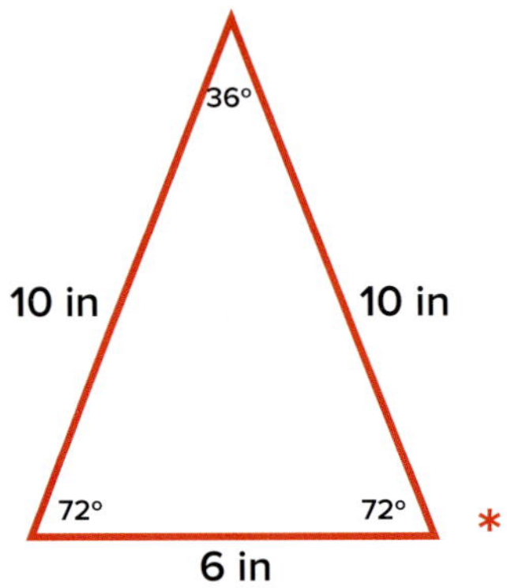

*Answer Key: Problem B

RIGHT ACUTE *or* OBTUSE *TRIANGLE*

If it seems tricky, start by figuring out the side classification. Look at the lengths of the sides; are any of them the same? If so, how many? If all three lengths are different, you know the triangle is scalene. If there are congruent sides, count them. Remember that two congruent sides make an isosceles triangle.

After you have named the triangle based on the sides, look at the angles. Pick out which angle is the biggest. If that angle is acute, then its measure will be less than 90 degrees. The two smaller angles must also equal less than 90 degrees for a triangle to be acute. If the biggest angle is 90 degrees, you have a right triangle. If it is larger than 90 degrees, then

“the interior angles OF A TRIANGLE ARE two right angles”

you have an obtuse triangle. Put your two classifications together and you will have completely named the triangle!

Do you think you could make a triangle that has two right angles? What about a triangle with two obtuse angles? As you imagine what such triangles might look like, you probably start to realize that they would be impossible. You would be right! If there were two right angles, that would sum to 180 degrees before adding the third angle. And two obtuse angles would be more than 180 degrees. As Euclid explains, “the interior angles of a triangle are two right angles.” That means there are always exactly 180 degrees in a triangle. But how do we *know* that this is true?

One thing mathematicians love to do is prove ideas. Sometimes these proofs involve a lot of writing and complicated explanations. However, to prove that there are 180 degrees inside a triangle, you don’t need any words at all.

First, cut out a triangle of any size. Because you are proving an idea that holds true for every triangle, if doesn’t matter how big or small your triangle is. Next, tear off the three corners so that you have the angles in front of you. Can you arrange these angles to make a different shape that you know has 180 degrees?

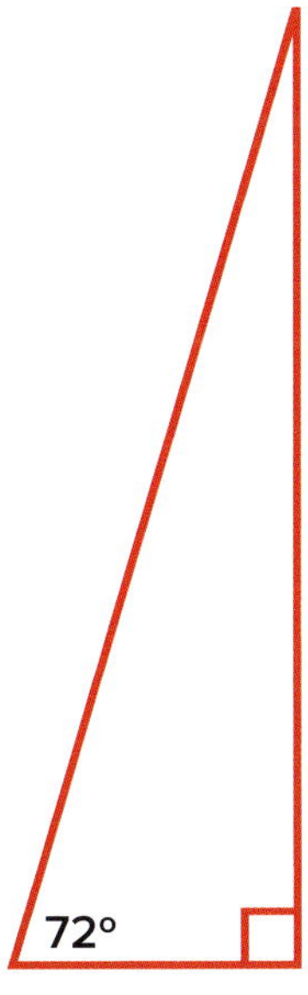

If you answered “yes,” then you noticed that you can turn the three angles of your triangle into a line. Together, the three angles have the same measure as a line—180 degrees! You can use this fact to solve problems with triangles. Knowing the measure of two angles will help you find the third angle because all three must add up to 180 degrees. Look at the triangle shown at left to see how this is done.

In that right triangle shown, how many degrees is the third angle? If you remember, the box in the corner of the bottom angle means that is 90 degrees. The two angles you know add up to 162 degrees. If you subtract that number from 180, then the last angle should be 18 degrees. Don't forget to check your work: 90 + 72 + 18 = 180, so the answer is correct!

See if you can find the measure of the missing angle in the problems below. Check your answers to see if you were right. Do your triangles equal exactly 180 degrees?

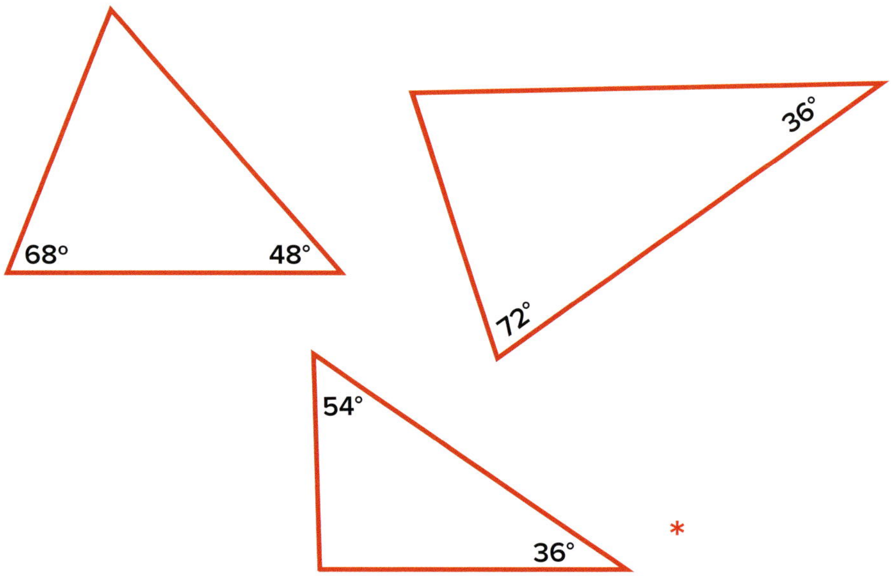

Besides knowing that there are 180 degrees in every triangle, there is another important **theorem** you should remember. It is called the Pythagorean theorem, and it works for only right triangles. This theorem shows that a special relationship exists among the legs of a right triangle (the sides next to the right angle) and the hypotenuse (the side across from the right angle). The theorem is named after the Greek mathematician Pythagoras. He founded a special club called the Pythagorean Brotherhood for people who were interested in learning. One thing the Brotherhood studied was this special triangular relationship.

**Answer Key: Problem C*

FIGURE IT OUT!

Euclidean Triangles

Isosceles triangles are defined as having two congruent sides. The angles across from those congruent sides are also congruent. Therefore, an isosceles triangle also has two congruent angles. This is a special theorem in Euclid's work. Mathematics students at Yale University had to prove this theorem before they could progress to higher levels of math. Once they mastered it, the students thrust a burning stick through Euclid's book to show that they had "gone through" Euclid!

The Pythagorean theorem says that the **square** of the length of one leg plus the square of the length of the other leg is equal to the hypotenuse squared. From the time this theorem was introduced, around 500 B.C., to the late 1500s, mathematicians wrote all their **equations** out with words, leading to long sentences like the former. However, you have probably seen the Pythagorean theorem written as $a^2 + b^2 = c^2$. This way of writing the equation developed only after French scholar François Viète introduced the idea of using letters to represent unknown quantities. The letters *a*, *b*, and *c* are thus **variables** for the different sides of the triangle. The letters *a* and *b* are the two legs; *c* is always the hypotenuse!

At some point in a math class, you will probably be asked to find the length of the missing side of a triangle. Sometimes that side will be a hypotenuse, but other times it will be a leg. As long as you substitute the correct term with the known quantity, you will be able to solve the problem without too much fuss.

Here's how you would solve for the hypotenuse (*c*), if you knew that the two legs were six and eight inches long:

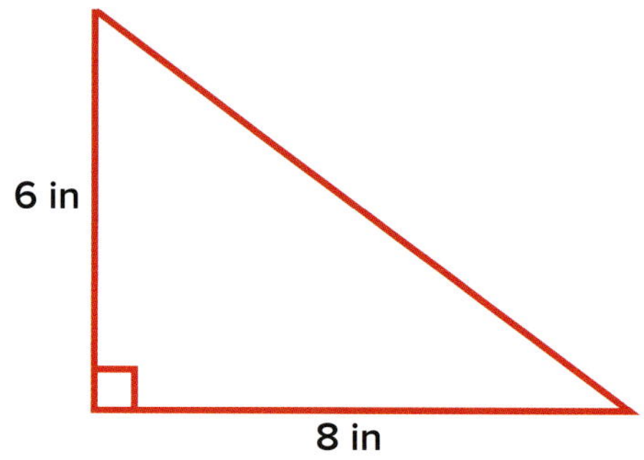

$a^2 + b^2 = c^2$ Start by writing out the Pythagorean theorem.

$6^2 + 8^2 = c^2$ Substitute the length of each leg for *a* and *b*, as *c* is the one that is missing.

$36 + 64 = c^2$ A number squared means times itself: $6^2 = 6 \cdot 6 = 36$.

$100 = c^2$ Add those two numbers together.

$10 = c$ Take the square root of both sides to get *c* by itself.

The length of the hypotenuse in this triangle is 10 inches.

And here is how you would solve for a leg, if you knew the length of the other, plus the length of the hypotenuse (the side across from the right angle):

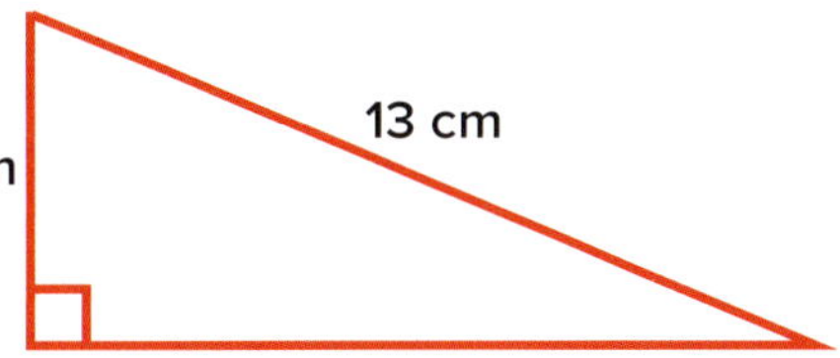

$a^2 + b^2 = c^2$	**Start with the formula again.**
$5^2 + b^2 = 13^2$	**Substitute the known lengths, including the length across from the right angle.**
$25 + b^2 = 169$	**Square the numbers that you can!**
$-25 \quad -25$	**Subtract 25 from both sides so that you can get *b* by itself.**
$b^2 = 144$	**Simplify 169 - 25. On the left side, the 25 canceled out.**
$b = 12$	**Finish by taking the square root of both sides.**

The length of the missing leg is 12 centimeters.

The Pythagorean theorem works for every right triangle. See if you can calculate the missing sides for the triangles below. Remember to substitute carefully, especially with the hypotenuse! One of the most common mistakes people make is substituting the letters into the incorrect places in the equation. To help yourself, write the letters next to each side of the triangle to remember which ones will be plugged into *a, b,* or *c*. Choose *a* to be the shortest leg and *b* to be the other leg; *c* is always the hypotenuse.

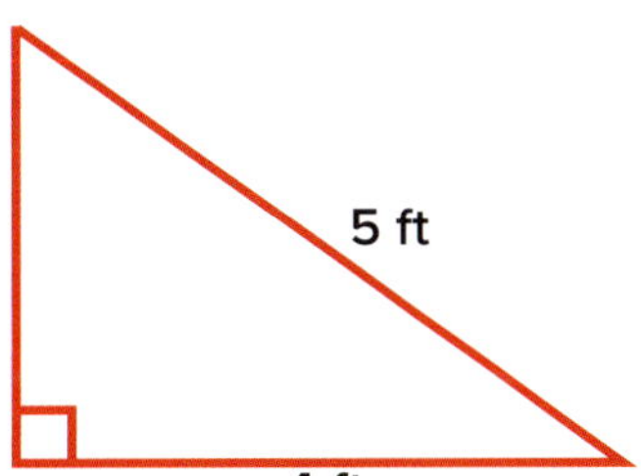

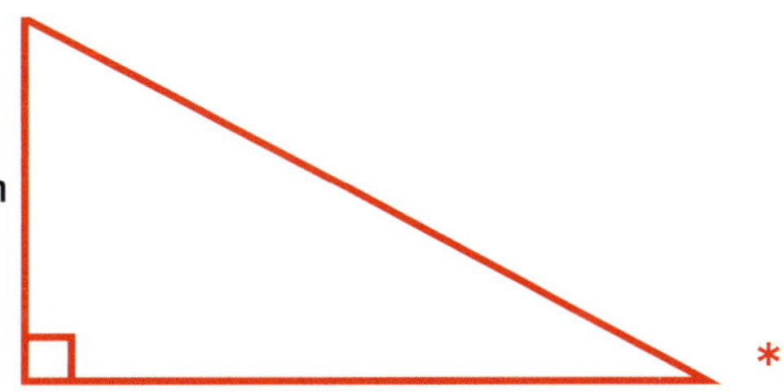

Pretty soon, the Pythagorean theorem will become like second nature to you. Remember that it only works for right triangles, though. For all triangles, you can identify the angles' measures based on the fact that every triangle has 180 degrees. That idea is important, even for polygons that have more sides! Don't forget about it.

**Answer Key: Problem D*

REGULAR SHAPES, IRREGULAR NAMES

IF YOU LOOK AT THE WORLD AROUND YOU, YOU WILL SEE THAT LINES, RAYS, segments, and triangles are not the only shapes out there. From where you are sitting right now, how many other shapes can you see?

You probably spotted all different kinds. Shapes with four sides, shapes with five sides—maybe even some with eight or more sides. It's important to know about those other shapes, too, because they can be encountered anywhere, and they help us understand shapes of any number of sides.

Just as you can classify triangles based on the lengths of their sides and the measures of their angles, you can name and classify shapes based on their similar features. Mathematicians name shapes for the number of sides or angles they have (for all shapes, the number of sides is equal to the number of angles). A three-sided figure is a triangle. A four-sided shape is a quadrilateral. These words rely on their

THREE-DIMENSIONAL QUADRILATERALS KNOWN AS CUBES HAVE SIX EQUAL SQUARES.

prefixes (the beginning parts of some words) to indicate number. For a triangle, the prefix *tri-* indicates three angles. In "quadrilateral," the prefix *quad-* means "four," while *-lateral* has to do with the sides.

Euclid used the word *polypleuron* ("many-sided") when writing about shapes with more than three sides. However, later mathematicians did not adopt Euclid's term. Rather, they settled into a pattern for the names of shapes by changing the prefix in front of *-gon*, which means "angled." For example, they used the prefix *penta-* to mean a shape with five angles, just like a person who competes in a pentathlon does five events. The names of shapes from 3 to 12 sides are listed below.

3 sides: triangle

4 sides: quadrilateral

5 sides: pentagon

6 sides: hexagon

7 sides: heptagon

8 sides: octagon

9 sides: nonagon

10 sides: decagon

11 sides: hendecagon

12 sides: dodecagon

PENTA
CONTA
KAIPEN
TAGON

According to the formula used on the shapes above, a shape with 55 sides would be pentacontakaipentagon. That would be a mouthful! As a result, when the number of sides increases past 12, mathematicians change course. First, they indicate the number of sides, and then they put *-gon* after it. So, a shape with 55 sides is really a 55-gon.

After naming a polygon for its number of sides, there are other ways you can describe it. Polygons can also be regular or irregular. For a polygon to be regular, all its angles must be the same measure, and all its sides must be the same length. If one of those requirements isn't met, a polygon can't be considered regular. It is irregular instead.

Polygons can also be described as being concave or convex. To check if a polygon is concave, draw in diagonals, or lines connecting the corners that are not next to one another. Do any of the lines go outside the shape? If they do, then the polygon is concave. A good way to remember the word "concave" and what it means is to think of your polygon as having a cave in it! If all the lines stay inside the shape, it is convex. Any polygon that is regular will always be convex.

Practice naming and describing the polygons below. Use the number of sides to come up with the names. Then describe the shapes as regular or irregular and concave or convex.

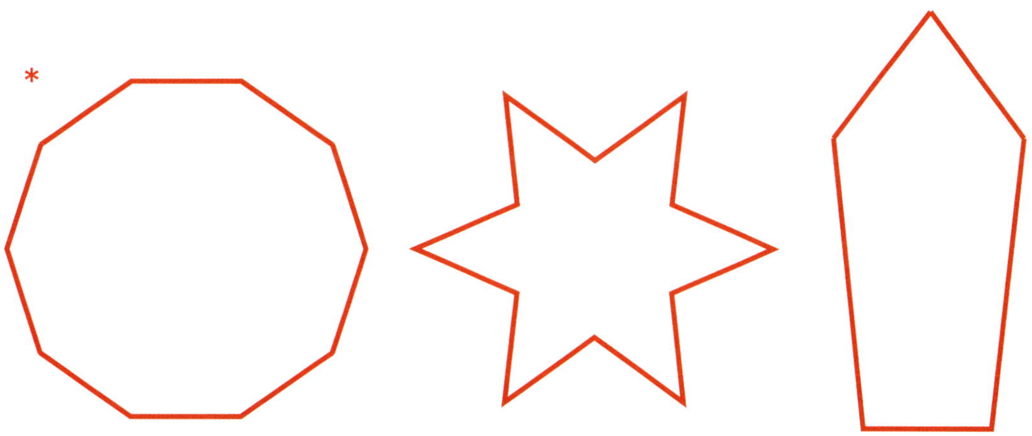

Now imagine any type of polygon that you want. What if you wanted to draw an irregular, concave 100-gon? It would take a lot of time and probably a lot of paper. Have you seen many of those shapes in your life? Probably not.

The most common shapes, other than triangles and circles, are quadrilaterals. Shapes such as parallelograms, rectangles, rhombuses, and squares are all different types of quadrilaterals. In fact, they are all known as special quadrilaterals!

Answer Key: Problem E

The most basic of those shapes is the parallelogram. A parallelogram is a quadrilateral whose opposite sides are parallel. Parallelograms have five special properties, which are listed below. They are true for and can be found in every parallelogram:

Opposite sides are parallel.

Opposite sides are congruent.

Opposite angles are congruent.

Consecutive angles (angles that share a side) are supplementary, meaning their angles add up to 180 degrees.

Diagonals bisect each other, which means the diagonals cut each other perfectly in half.

You can make use of those properties to solve different problems involving parallelograms. Each property is used once in the problems below. See if you can figure out the missing information for each picture, based on what you *do* know.

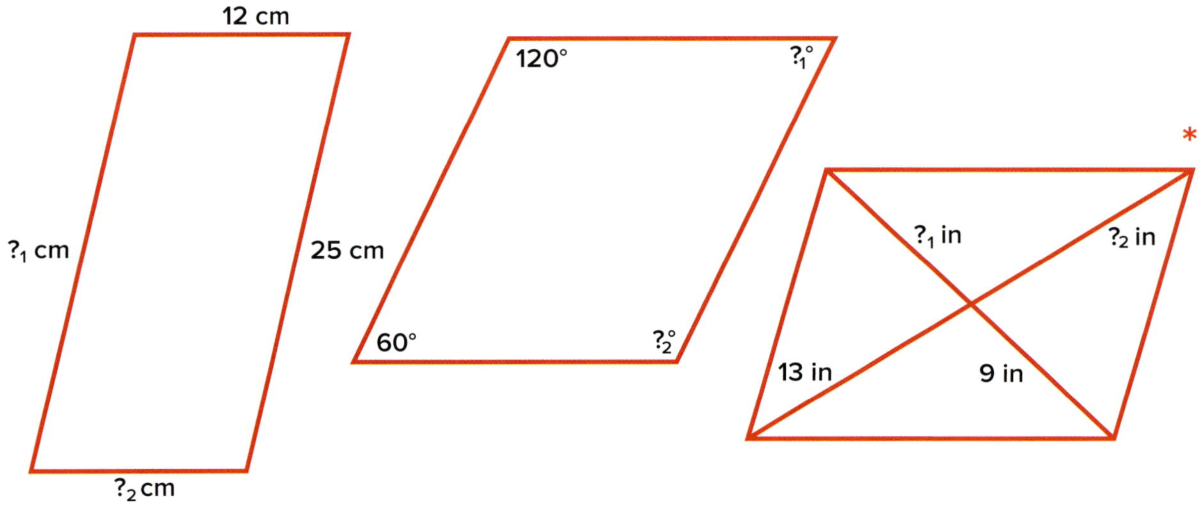

What if, in a parallelogram, you made all the angles congruent? None of the other properties would need to change. Because the angles of a quadrilateral add up to 360 degrees on the inside of a quadrilateral, each

**Answer Key: Problem F*

angle in your new shape would have to be 90 degrees (360÷4). Therefore, that shape would be a rectangle. Rectangles are parallelograms with four congruent angles. Rectangles share all the properties of parallelograms, plus they have congruent angles and diagonals.

Now what if we went back to the parallelogram that became a rectangle and, instead of making all the angles congruent, the four *sides* became congruent? The new shape should look kind of like a diamond. A mathematician would call this shape a rhombus. Rhombuses are quadrilaterals with four congruent sides. They, like rectangles, have the same properties of the original parallelogram. But unlike rectangles, they also include the following properties:

All sides are congruent.
Diagonals are perpendicular.
Diagonals bisect opposite angles.

Here is where parallelograms get exciting. Look at rectangles and rhombuses; neither of those two shapes is regular. They could be considered half regular, since they each meet one of the criteria, but such a distinction wouldn't fly with serious mathematicians. However, if you were to combine the two definitions and make a parallelogram that has all angles and all sides congruent, you would get a square, the only regular quadrilateral. This relationship among parallelograms, rectangles, rhombuses, and squares can be represented using the following **Venn diagram**.

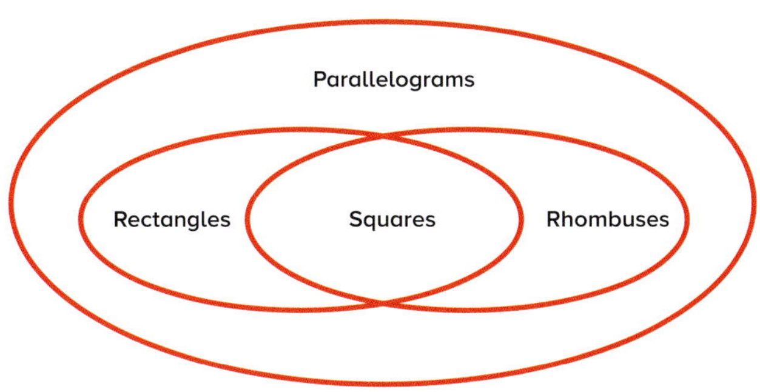

THESE PROPERTIES *CAN HELP* YOU SOLVE *PROBLEMS*

The list of special quadrilaterals goes on. Trapezoids are quadrilaterals that have only one pair of parallel sides. Within the group of trapezoids, there is another division. Isosceles trapezoids are trapezoids whose non-parallel sides are congruent. Take a closer look at isosceles trapezoids and their specific properties.

There is one pair of parallel sides.

One pair of opposite sides is congruent.

Diagonals are congruent.

Base angles (the angles at the top and bottom of a trapezoid) are congruent.

Those properties can help you solve problems with isosceles trapezoids. However, there is another theorem for all trapezoids that also appears. In a trapezoid, if you connect the midpoint—the point positioned exactly in the middle of a segment—of one leg to the midpoint of the other, the midsegment is formed. In a trapezoid, the midsegment is parallel to the bases, and the length of the midsegment is the average of the lengths of the bases.

In other words, the length of the midsegment is equal to one-half of the quantity of the length of the top base plus the length of the bottom base. Using this formula, calculate the length of the missing segments of the trapezoids shown on the next page. The first one is done for you!

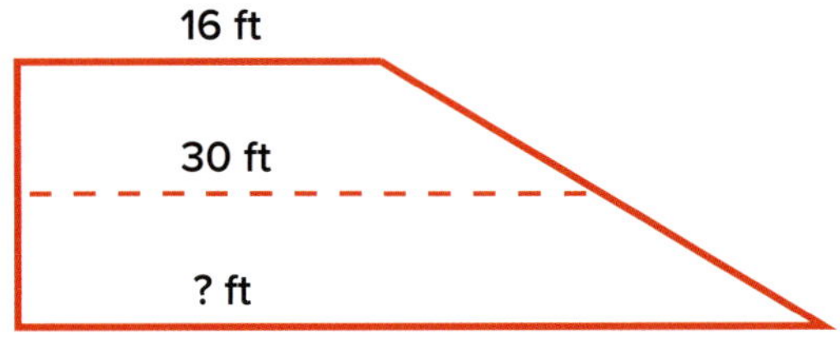

midsegment **=**

½(top + bottom)	**Start by writing out the formula.**
30 = ½(16 + ?)	**Substitute the values for the three known segments.**
60 = 16 + ?	**Multiply both sides by two and clear out the fraction.**
- 16 - 16	**Subtract 16 from each side. You are done!**
44 = ?	**Simplify 60 - 16.**

The bottom base is 44 feet long.

As you solve the rest of the problems, you can check your work by comparing your answer with the other two segments. Is the midsegment length you calculated a value between the lengths of the two bases?

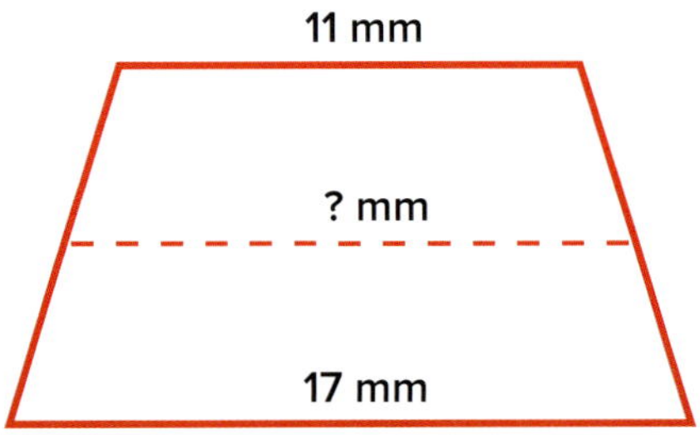

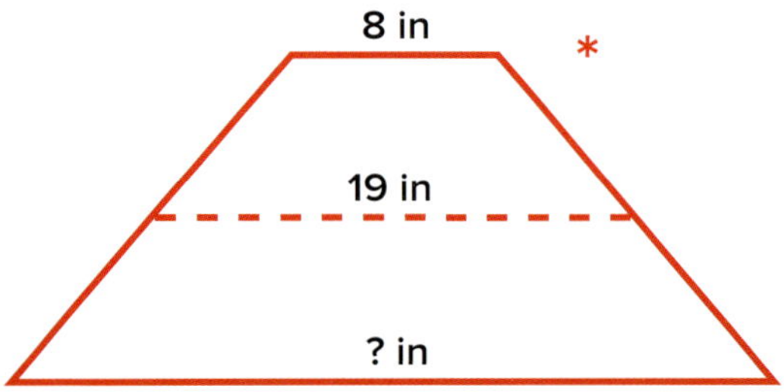

Quadrilaterals continue to appear as you move into more challenging areas of math. In fact, even in **calculus**, when you begin working with finding area under a specific curve, rectangles and trapezoids appear. They can also be found in the world around us. Trapezoids act as the structure for many bridges. Being able to calculate the midsegment and work with other trapezoid properties is important for engineers who work to make those bridges safe. It's amazing what can be done with quadrilaterals!

**Answer Key: Problem G*

FIGURE IT OUT!

Geometric Puzzles

Tangrams are geometric puzzles made of seven polygons: two large isosceles right triangles, one medium isosceles right triangle, two small isosceles right triangles, a square, and a parallelogram. Solving the puzzle involves recreating a specific shape given only an outline. Tangrams originated in China during the Song dynasty, approximately 1,000 years ago. In the 19th century, the puzzles spread to Europe, and since then, more than 6,000 tangrams have been generated.

PI, THE NUMBER FOR CIRCLES

LINES AND THEIR PIECES CAN BE USED TO GENERATE THE POLYGONS FOUND IN THE WORLD AROUND YOU. Yet for Euclid, all those shapes were only half of his work. If you recall, his work was based on two shapes: the line and the circle. We have already defined a line to be a straight path that goes forever. How would you describe what a circle is? You might use phrases such as "no corners" or "round."

Mathematicians like to be exact when they define terms, and that goes for circles as well. A mathematician would define a circle as the set of all points that are the same distance from a given point.

From this definition come the definitions of some other words having to do with circles. For example, the radius of a circle is the distance from a given point, called the center, to the edge of the circle. The diameter

THE GEOMETRICAL NAME FOR A RING-SHAPED DOUGHNUT IS A TORUS.

is two times the radius. It is a segment that goes from one side of the circle to the other while passing through the center. *Diameter* and *radius* show up in many of the calculations that mathematicians do with circles.

There is also an important number associated with circles. Pi (π) is defined as the **ratio** of the **circumference** of a circle to its diameter. It was the subject of many of the first calculations that mathematicians did with circles. Pi is an irrational number, a number that cannot be written as a fraction. That means that pi never stops. You can list as many digits as you want, but there is always another one to find. There are infinitely many digits of pi.

If all the digits of pi are still not known, you may be wondering how mathematicians thousands of years ago were able to discover any of them. One mathematician in particular, Archimedes of Sicily, studied circles and pi by using polygons. First, he drew a circle. He then put a hexagon inside the circle, fitting it perfectly so that it touched the circle with every corner. He also drew a hexagon around the circle, fitting the circle inside the hexagon, so that the circle touched each side of it. For each hexagon, Archimedes was able to calculate the perimeter, or the distance around the outside. He knew the circumference measure would be between those two measures, and since he knew the radius, he was able to approximate pi. He improved the accuracy of his approximation by doubling the hexagon to make a 12-gon, a 24-gon, a 48-gon, and finally a 96-gon. Then he was able to calculate the first four digits of pi.

Fortunately, thanks to the work of Archimedes and other mathematicians, you don't need to go through all that to use pi in your own calculations. Calculators have pi stored on them, so you just need to push the **π** button. Most calculators have up to 15 digits of pi. If you were to use an extremely powerful computer for your homework, then

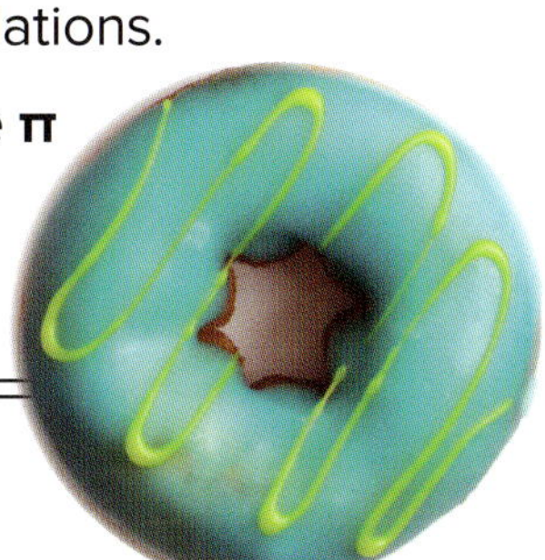

you would have access to the more than 10 trillion digits of pi that have been found. However, as you perform calculations with pi, you won't need even that many—3.14 is often all it takes.

You use pi, just as Archimedes did, to calculate the circumference and area of a circle. To figure out the circumference, mathematicians use the formula $C=2\pi r$. Because the diameter is equal to two times the radius, the formula can also be thought of as $C=\pi d$. To calculate the circumference, you need to plug in the values for each variable into the correct equation. For instance, if you know the radius, then use $C=2\pi r$. But if you know the diameter, use $C=\pi d$.

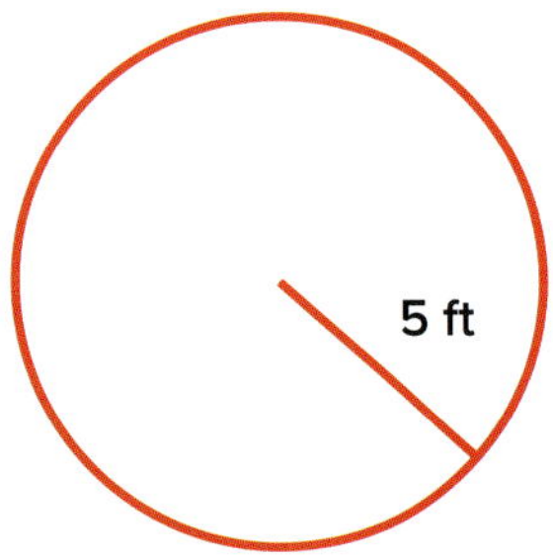

$C = 2\pi r$ Always start with the formula!

$C = 2\pi(5)$ Substitute 5 for the radius.

$C = 31.42$ Multiply 2 and 5. Calculate 10 times π. The answer is rounded to the nearest hundredth, or two decimal places. The circumference of this circle is 31.42 feet.

Try the following problems on your own. Be sure to calculate carefully.

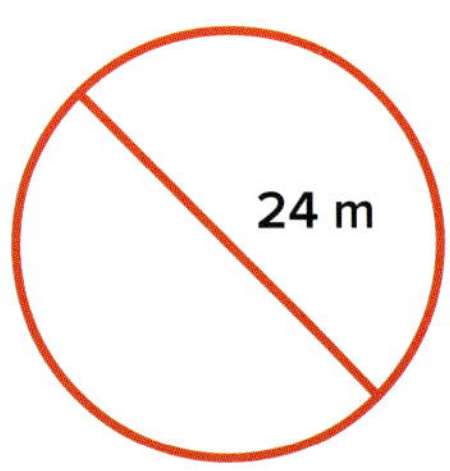

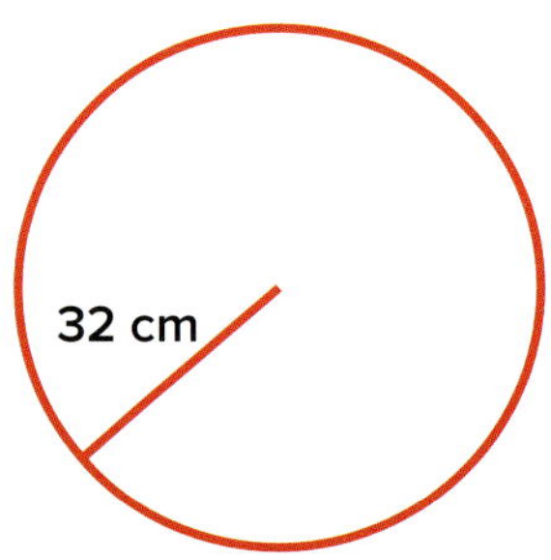

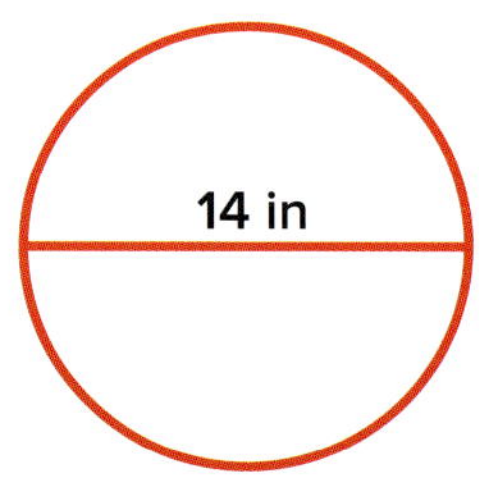

*

Mathematicians also use pi to calculate a circle's area, or the amount of space a shape takes up. The formula to do this is $A=\pi r^2$. Area can be found with the same steps used for circumference (except you won't ever use the length of the diameter). You will start by substituting in the length of the radius. Look at the picture carefully! If the diameter is given, you will need to divide by two before plugging the value into the formula. Calculate the area of the circles on page 38. There is an example done for you.

**Answer Key: Problem H*

FIGURE IT OUT!

Between Dimensions

Did you know that there is a dimensional figure between the one-dimensional line and two-dimensional circles and polygons? Fractals fall into this in-between space. They are figures that have self-similarity, meaning that each part of the shape has the same pattern as the whole. They were first formalized as mathematicians examined snowflakes and shorelines. The ideas of self-similarity and fractional dimension are what make these shapes different from Euclid's shapes.

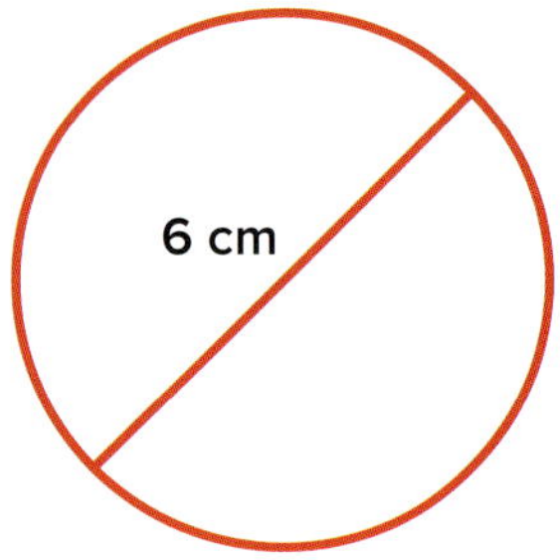

$A = \pi r^2$	**Start with the formula.**
$A = \pi(3)^2$	**Because the diameter is given as six, divide by two to get a radius of three.**
$A = 28.27$	**Do the calculations and get your answer! The area of the circle is 28.27 cm^2.**

Now it's your turn to try a few:

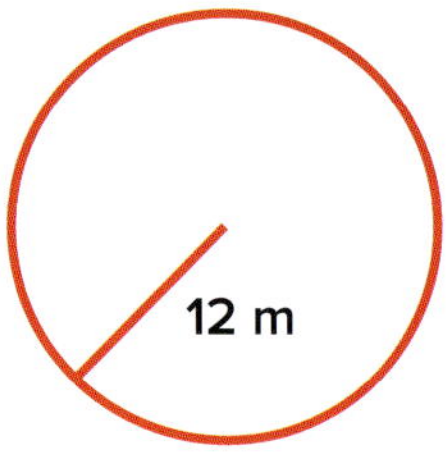

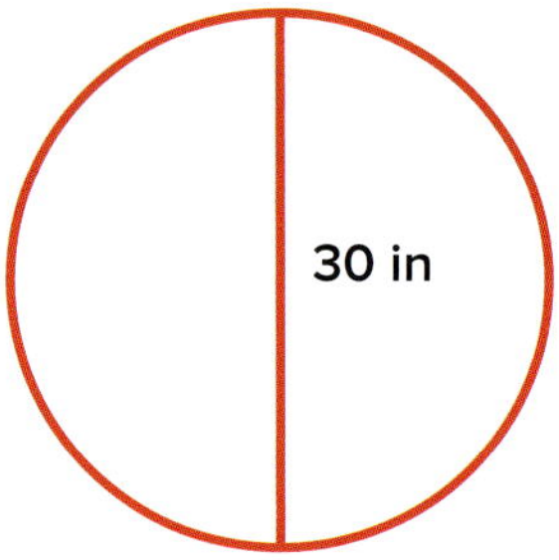

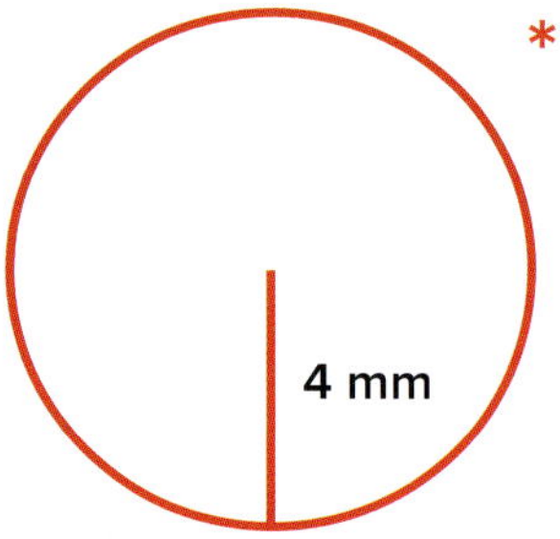

*

Did you notice that in the examples above, all the units were written with a number to the second power on them? Remember that for area, you are calculating the two-dimensional space inside a shape. To do that, you multiply the radius by itself. The units on the radius also multiply, meaning they are squared as well. For example, cm · cm is written as cm^2. If you have trouble remembering how to write the units for area, think of the fact that you are doing math for a two-dimensional shape. That means your units will need to be to the second power.

You can also calculate the area of a portion of a circle. This piece, called a sector, is shaped like a slice of pie. Finding the area of the sector starts by finding the area of the entire circle. Then you determine the measure of the angle that the sector forms and divide it by the 360 degrees of the whole circle. Multiply that fraction (angle measure/360) by the area.

Such fractional amounts are also used to draw pie charts, which are graphs that represent percentages of a total as pieces of a "pie." If you can turn the percentage into a fraction out of 360, you will know how big to make a particular sector. Look at the following example problem for further review.

**Answer Key: Problem I*

A survey was conducted of 180 seventh-graders. When asked what their favorite school lunch was, 81 students answered pizza, 45 students responded that they brought their lunch from home, 27 said spaghetti, 20 answered salad, and 7 said turkey with mashed potatoes. What would these findings look like on a pie chart?

First, you will need to calculate how many degrees each group takes up. For pizza, $81/180$ is 45 percent, or 0.45. If you take 0.45 times 360, you get 162 degrees, the amount of the chart needed for the pizza sector. Doing the same process for each of the other answers gives 90 degrees for bringing lunches from home, 54 degrees for spaghetti, 40 degrees for salad, and 14 degrees for turkey and potatoes.

You can use a protractor to draw each of the angles in the circle. By labeling each sector with the name of the food, you have used a circle to represent the information in the survey. The graph quickly shows you that almost half the students like pizza! It also shows you that not many people enjoy the turkey and mashed potatoes option.

Seventh-Grade Lunch Choices

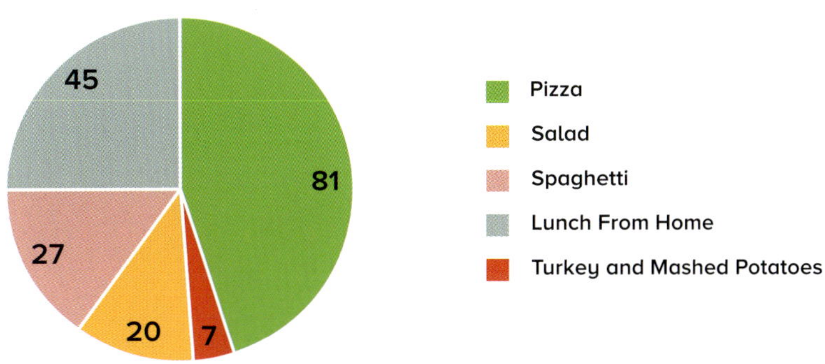

It's amazing how many different problems you can solve simply by using shapes such as circles. Mathematicians have come a long way from the days of Euclid. But considering that even he had 465 ideas about math, there will always be more to discover in this wide-ranging branch of mathematics called geometry!

MATH TOOLKIT

1. Shapes are at the heart of geometry. Therefore, when you have a word problem that involves geometric ideas, it is helpful to draw a diagram. When working with a word problem, in addition to identifying important numbers and their descriptions, you should also look for words that give you clues on what to draw. (Often, the specific shape will not be named.) Once you have drawn a figure, be sure to label it with any numbers that it may require.

2. There is an easy way to check your answers when working with the Pythagorean theorem. In any right triangle, the hypotenuse is the longest side, and it is across from the right angle. The "Goldilocks rule" of right triangles states that the longest side is opposite the largest angle, and the shortest side is opposite the smallest angle. When you finish a problem, go back and write the answer you found onto the picture. Then check the lengths of the sides with the angles across from them. Do they follow the "Goldilocks rule"?

3. To calculate the measure of the interior angles of any polygon, first divide the shape into triangles. Then multiply the number of triangles by 180 degrees. That will give you the number of degrees in that shape. Because there are always two fewer triangles than the number of sides, there is also a formula that can be used: The interior angle sum is equal to the number of sides (n) minus 2 multiplied by 180 degrees, or $(n - 2) \cdot 180^\circ$.

4. So when does a line become a shape? If you cut a line into pieces, new shapes could be formed. You could make nearly every shape imaginable, except for one: circles can be drawn only with a compass. This tool rotates a writing utensil around a point, drawing a curved path that is always the same distance from that point. The lack of straight sides in a circle means that it is not the product of a line but something entirely different.

GLOSSARY

calculations: operations performed on numbers

calculus: a branch of mathematics that studies change, usually on an infinitely small level

circumference: the distance around the outside of a circle

classify: to put objects into categories based on certain characteristics

common notions: statements about numbers that Euclid believed to be obvious

congruent: two shapes that have the same size; identical

equations: math sentences that connect two equal expressions, which are combinations of numbers, variables, and operations

fraction: a number that relates pieces of a whole quantity by division

polygons: closed figures with straight sides that do not overlap

protractor: a tool used for measuring angles

ratio: a comparison of two quantities through division

square: a number multiplied by itself; represented with an exponent of two

square root: a number that when multiplied by itself gives back an original number; for example, three is the square root of nine, three times three is nine

theorem: a mathematical statement that has been proven

variables: letters that are used to represent unknown quantities

Venn diagram: a diagram that shows the relationship between two or more sets through the use of overlapping circles

SELECTED BIBLIOGRAPHY

Berlinghoff, William P., and Fernando Q. Gouvêa. *Math through the Ages: A Gentle History for Teachers and Others.* Washington, D.C.: MAA Service Center, 2004.

Euclid. *The First Six Books of the Elements of Euclid.* Edited by John Casey. Reprint of the 1885 Dublin edition, Project Gutenberg, 2007. http://www.gutenberg.org/files/21076/21076-pdf.pdf.

O'Connor, John J., and Edmund F. Robertson. "A History of Pi." MacTutor History of Mathematics Archive. http://www-history.mcs.st-andrews.ac.uk/HistTopics/Pi_through_the_ages.html.

Rooney, Anne. *The Story of Mathematics.* London: Arcturus, 2008.

Struik, Dirk J. *A Concise History of Mathematics.* New York: Dover, 1987.

Thomsen, D. E. "Fractals: Magical Fun or Revolutionary Science?" *Science News*, vol. 131 (1987): 184.

WEBSITES

Geometry Math Games
http://www.math-play.com/Geometry-Math-Games.html
This website has a bunch of different math games about geometry.

NOVA: Approximating Pi
http://www.pbs.org/wgbh/nova/physics/approximating-pi.html
This website lets you pick different polygons so that you can recreate Archimedes's process for finding pi.

Note: Every effort has been made to ensure that the websites listed above are suitable for children, that they have educational value, and that they contain no inappropriate material. However, because of the nature of the Internet, it is impossible to guarantee that these sites will remain active indefinitely or that their contents will not be altered.

INDEX

ANSWER KEY

Problem A

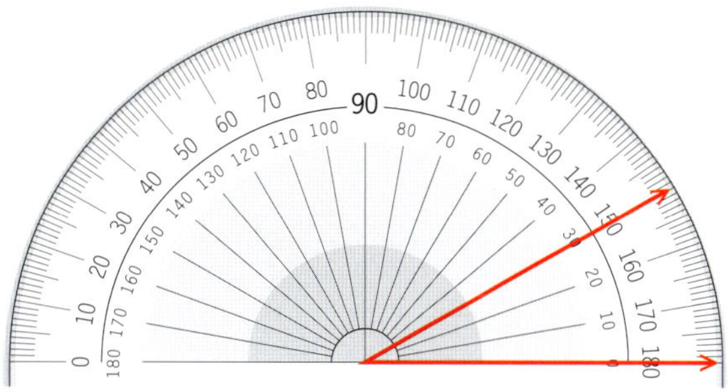

The angle is acute, so between the two choices of 30 or 150 degrees, the answer must be 30 degrees.

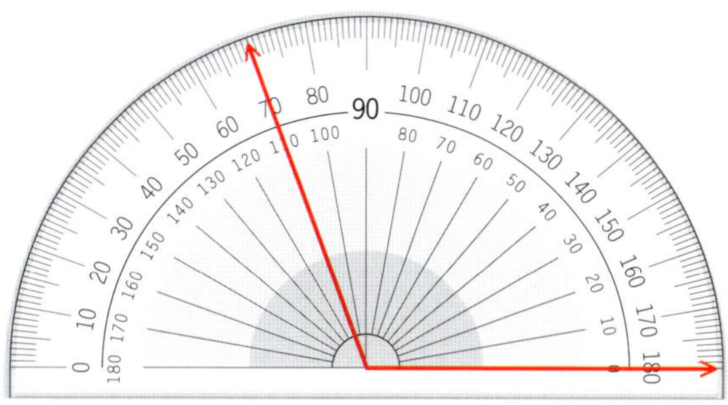

The angle is obtuse, so between the two choices of 70 or 110 degrees, the angle must measure 110 degrees.

Problem B

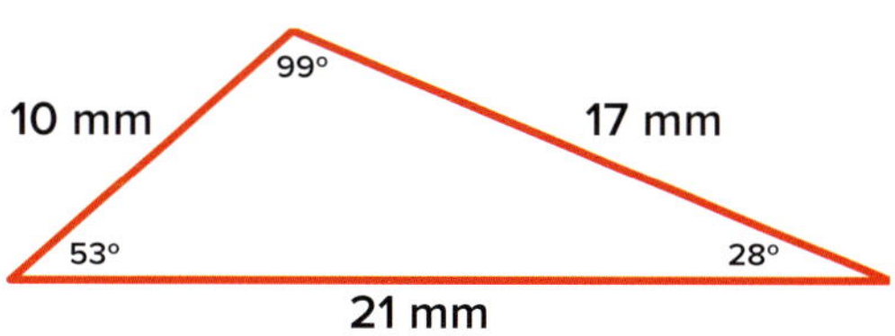

scalene, obtuse

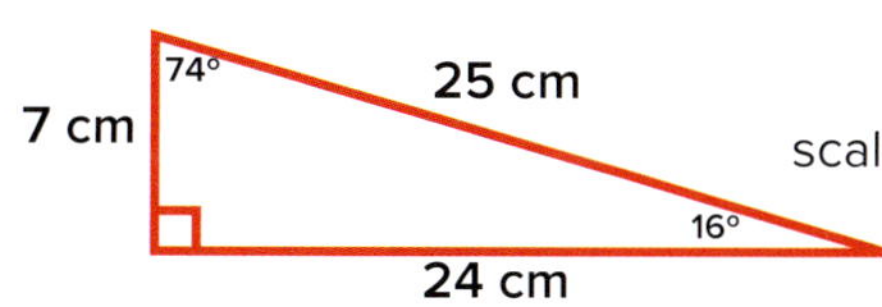

scalene, right

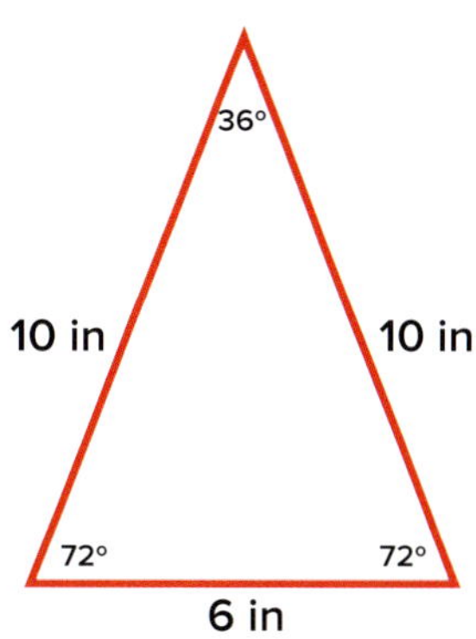

isosceles, acute

Problem C

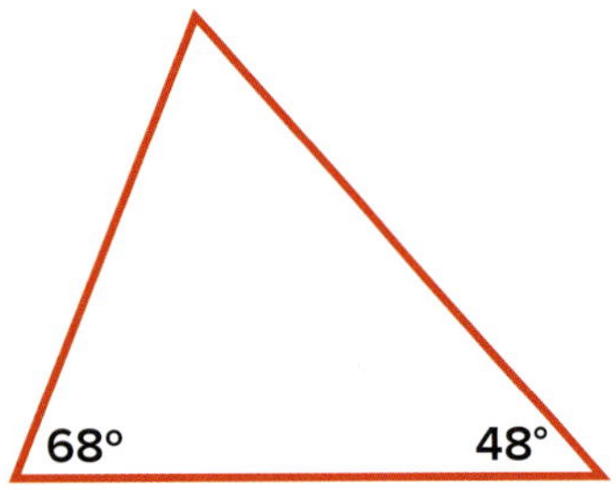

$68° + 48° + \text{missing angle} = 180°$
$116° + \text{missing angle} = 180°$
$\text{missing angle} = 64°$

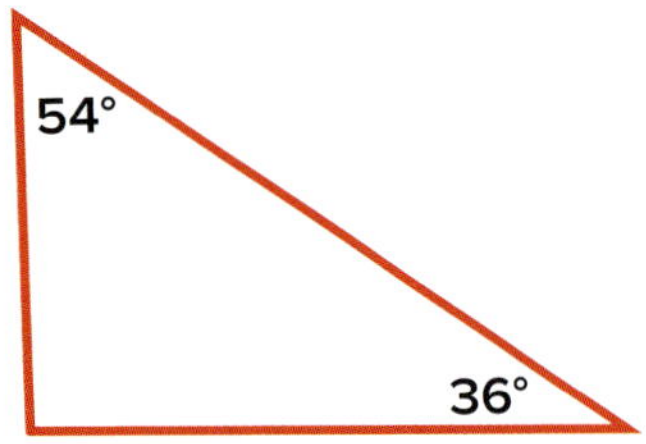

$54° + 36° + \text{missing angle} = 180°$
$90° + \text{missing angle} = 180°$
$\text{missing angle} = 90°$

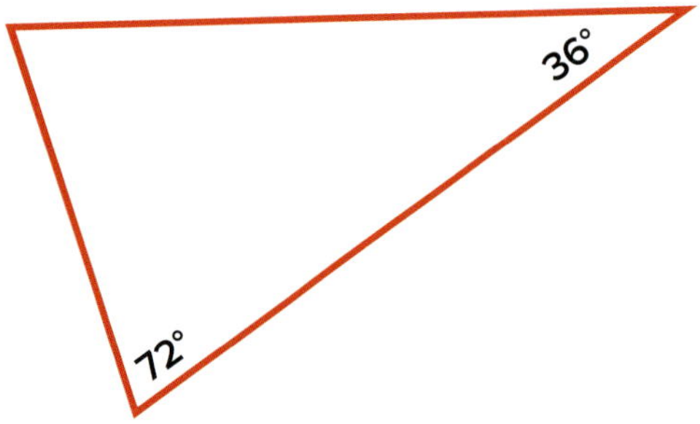

$72° + 36° + \text{missing angle} = 180°$
$108° + \text{missing angle} = 180°$
$\text{missing angle} = 72°$

Problem D

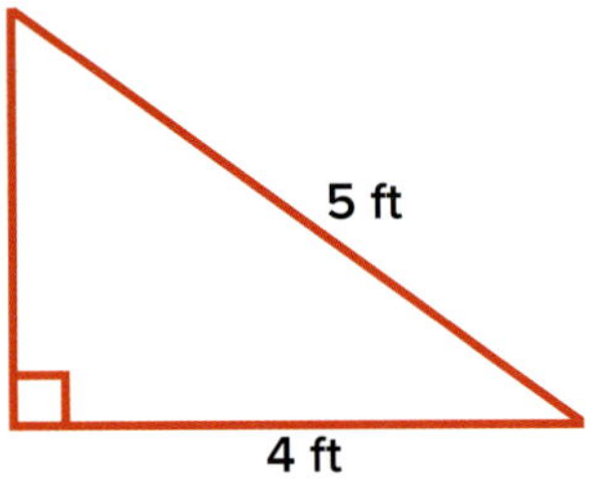

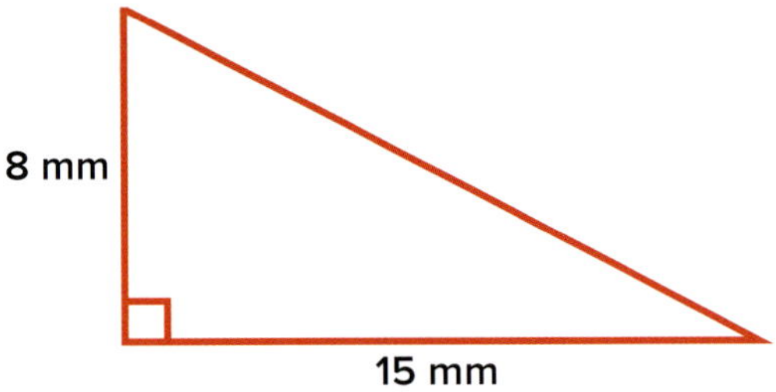

$a^2 + b^2 = c^2$
$a^2 + 4^2 = 5^2$
$a^2 + 16 = 25$
$a^2 = 9$
$a = 3$

$a^2 + b^2 = c^2$
$8^2 + 15^2 = c^2$
$64 + 225 = c^2$
$289 = c^2$
$17 = c$

Problem E

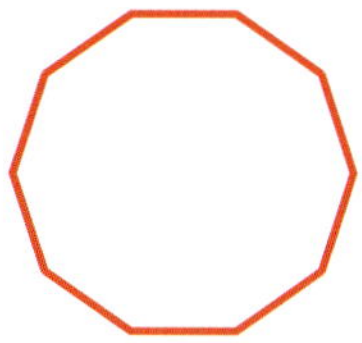

decagon,
regular, convex

dodecagon,
irregular, concave

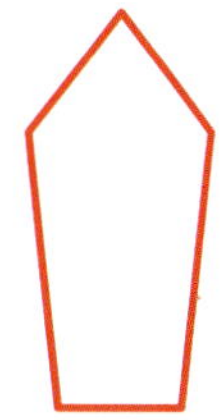

pentagon,
irregular, convex

Problem F

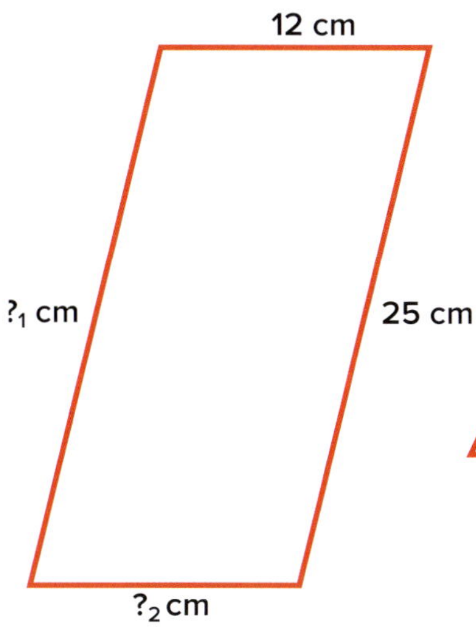

$?_1$: 25 cm (opposite sides are congruent)
$?_2$: 12 cm (opposite sides are congruent)

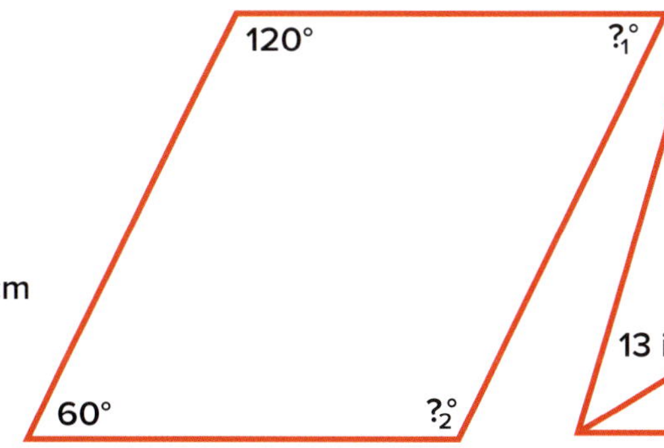

$?_1$: 60 degrees (opposite angles are congruent)
$?_2$: 120 degrees (opposite angles are congruent)

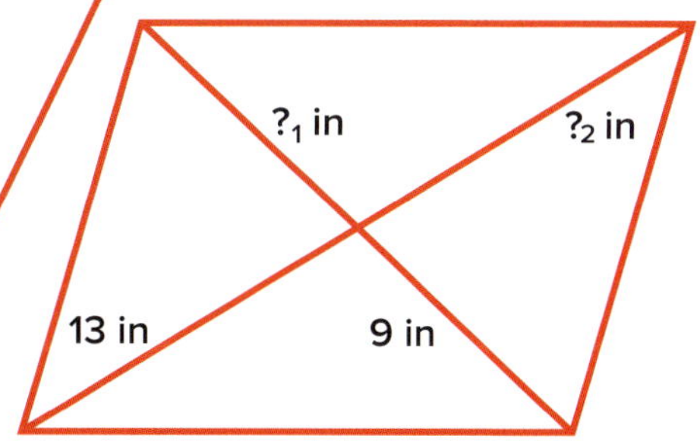

$?_1$: 9 in (diagonals bisect each other)
$?_2$: 13 in (diagonals bisect each other)

Problem G

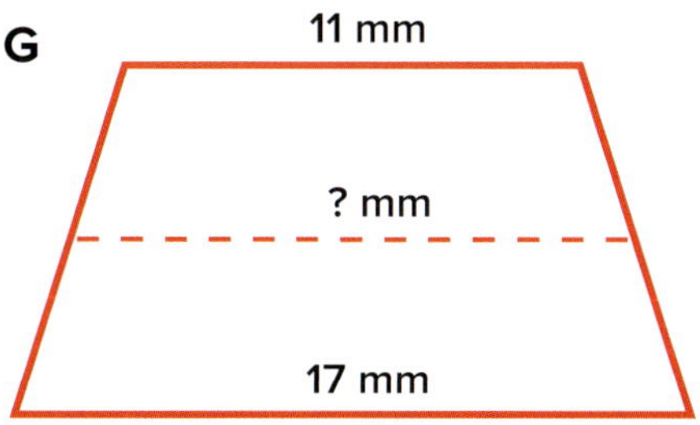

midsegment = ½(top + bottom)
? = ½(11 + 17)
? = ½(28)
? = 14

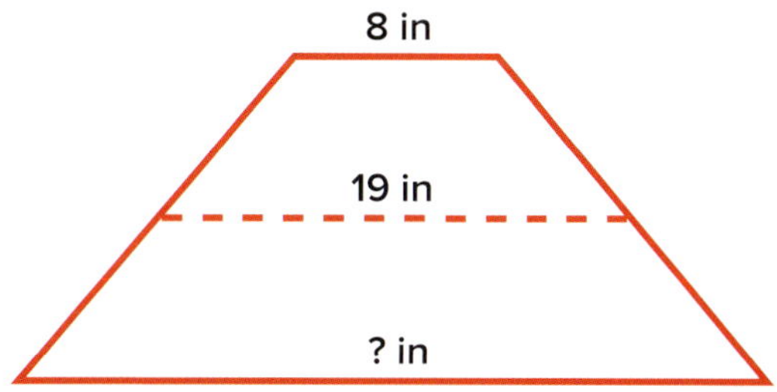

midsegment = ½(top + bottom)
19 = ½(8 + ?)
38 = 8 + ?
30 = ?

Problem H

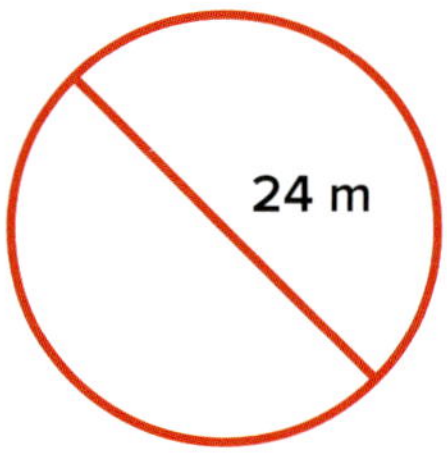

$C = \pi d$
$C = \pi(24)$
$C = 75.40$ m

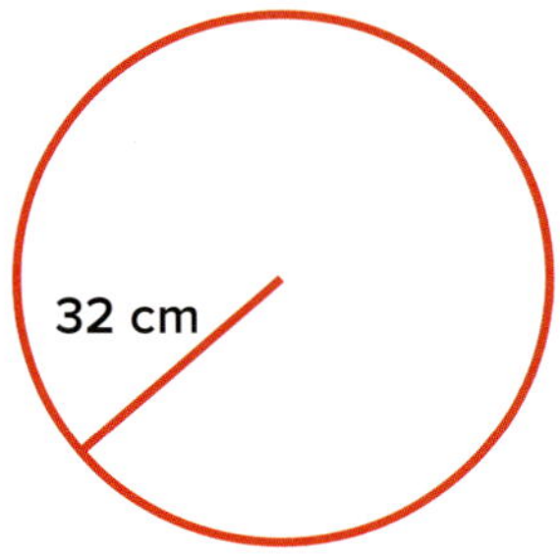

$C = 2\pi r$
$C = 2\pi(32)$
$C = 201.06$ cm

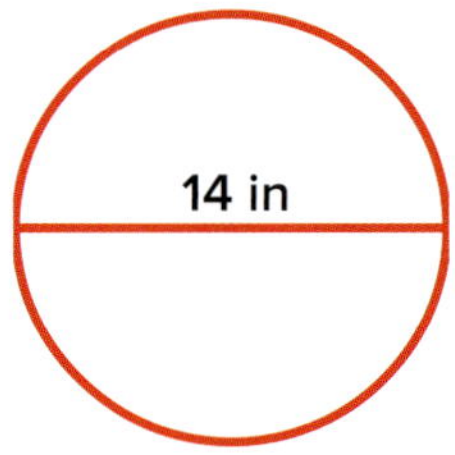

$C = \pi d$
$C = \pi(14)$
$C = 43.98$ in

Problem I

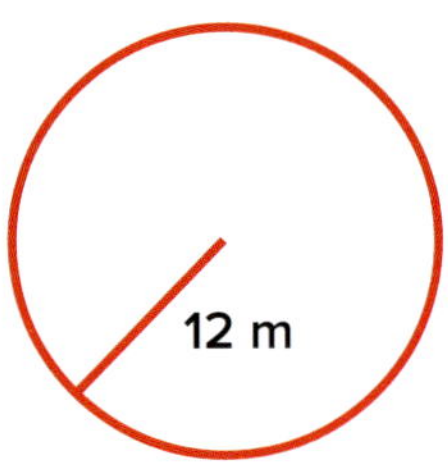

$A = \pi r^2$
$A = \pi(12)^2$
$A = 144\pi$
$A = 452.39$ m^2

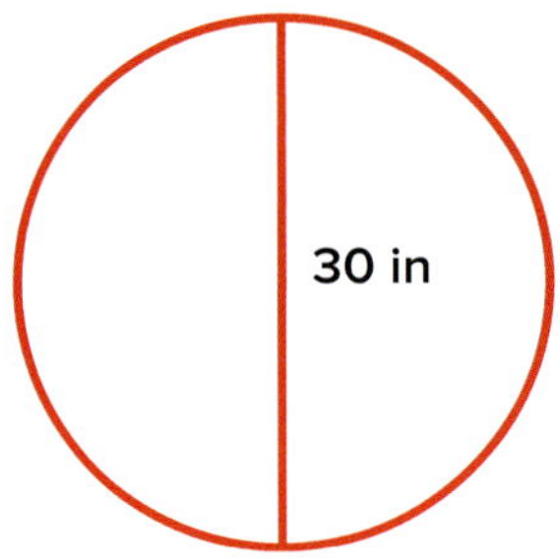

$A = \pi r^2$
$A = \pi(15)^2$
$A = 225\pi$
$A = 706.86$ in^2

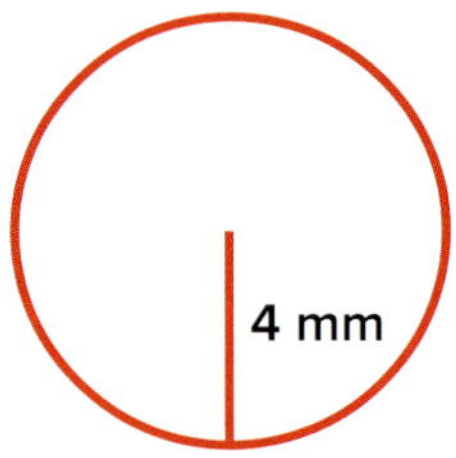

$A = \pi r^2$
$A = \pi(4)^2$
$A = 16\pi$
$A = 50.27$ mm^2